LATIMER STUDIES 74

DEIFICATION AND UNION WITH CHRIST

A REFORMED PERSPECTIVE ON SALVATION IN ORTHODOXY

BY SLAVKO EŽDENCI

The Latimer Trust

Deification and Union with Christ: A Reformed Perspective on Salvation in Orthodoxy © Slavko Eždenci 2011

ISBN   978-0-946307-81-4

Cover photo © PReckas – Fotolia.com

Published by the Latimer Trust June 2011

The Latimer Trust (formerly Latimer House, Oxford) is a conservative Evangelical research organisation within the Church of England, whose main aim is to promote the history and theology of Anglicanism as understood by those in the Reformed tradition. Interested readers are welcome to consult its website for further details of its many activities.

The Latimer Trust
PO Box 26685, London N14 4XQ UK
Registered Charity: 1084337
Company Number: 4104465
Web: www.latimertrust.org
E-mail: administrator@latimertrust.org

Contents

Preface

Before I describe and evaluate the concepts of deification and union with Christ, I have to acknowledge my Evangelical Reformed background. Without doubt this background influences both my approach and methodology in evaluating the concepts of deification and union with Christ.

On the other hand, I have to say that this is not just a pure 'academic' exercise since the Orthodox Church was at the beginning of my search for God. I attended Orthodox church services in Serbia for over a year and a half. During that time I was whole-heartedly trying to find the way to God and to understand the way of salvation in Orthodoxy. Also, during my time of theological studies in the UK, I had the opportunity to spend a month with devout believers in the Russian Orthodox Church in Cambridge. They were very welcoming and open to talk about their faith and I want to express gratitude to them for enabling me to appreciate Orthodoxy more. My intention with regards to Orthodoxy is thus to present deification primarily through the lens of Orthodox writers to my best knowledge and understanding.

I would like to thank Mike Ovey who supervised the short dissertation, of which this work is an expansion. His helpful comments enabled me to clarify my thoughts on the topic. Any errors remain my own.

Slavko Eždenci 2011

Introduction

The concept of deification, or union with God, is a distinctive mark of Orthodoxy. It has a central role within the Eastern theological framework. It was developed by the Greek Fathers and has been the focus of the Orthodox Church since Athanasius. Since among Western Protestants there has been a recent renewal of interest in Orthodoxy, it is not surprising that scholars are trying not just to rediscover deification, but also to identify deification in Western theology. Deification is consequently found by some in the works of leading Western theologians, such as Augustine, Aquinas, Luther, Calvin, and Jonathan Edwards.[1]

In contrast, with regards to salvation, the Western Church has focused on the cross, and since the Reformation, more specifically on justification by faith. Although within this theological framework the doctrine of union with Christ is considered essential for gaining salvation, it has often been neglected or not taught in it's full dimensions.[2]

This paper will thus examine these two key concepts in the Orthodox and Reformed traditions. Their comparison is worthwhile as it will illuminate their weaknesses and strengths. This will further lead towards practical application for teaching in Reformed churches as well as for dialogue with Orthodox Christians.

The scope of this paper will be limited in three ways. Firstly, this paper is primarily aimed at those within the Reformed tradition.

---

[1] Carl Mosser, "The greatest possible blessing: Calvin and deification," *Scottish Journal of Theology* 55 (2002): p 36.

[2] Gaffin points out that although Calvin has explained the significance of union with Christ, there has been a tendency to view union as largely legal in nature. Richard B. Gaffin, "Union with Christ: some biblical and theological reflections," in *Always Reforming: Exploration in systematic theology* (ed. A.T.B. McGowan; Leicester: IVP, 2006), p 271.

In order to help the reader evaluate the doctrine of deification but also to learn from it, the differences between these two doctrines will be presented from a Reformed point of view.

It must be acknowledged that any comparison of Reformed and Orthodox doctrine is restricted to some degree. Primarily we recognise that these doctrines are the result of two completely different historical and cultural backgrounds. This means that some important questions for the West, like the question of justification by faith for example, have never been the issues at stake for the East.

In addition to this, there is a difference in methodology and approach towards theology between Orthodox and Reformed Christians. While the Western mind-set tries to explain and rationalise everything, for some aspects of Orthodox faith it is enough to say: "It is a mystery."[3] However, this mysticism in Orthodoxy is not irrationalism and denial of the possibility to know God.

Moreover, Orthodox theology is integrated with worship. Ware explains that 'the Orthodox approach to religion is fundamentally a liturgical approach, which understands the doctrine in the context of divine worship.'[4] Thus, alongside doctrines, liturgy is also 'a major vehicle of teaching,'[5] and so some Orthodox belief is not explicitly described in a particular doctrine.

Given these differences, it is important to recognise that the applied methodology, comparison and evaluation in this paper come from the Reformed tradition.

Secondly, these concepts will be examined specifically with regards to the attainment of man's salvation. Deification is actually a broader concept which includes the whole of creation. The Orthodox position is that even before the fall, deification was the end and final fulfilment not just of humanity but of all created beings. Man's

---

[3]   Michael Harper, *A Faith Fulfilled: why are Christians across Great Britain embracing Orthodoxy?* (Ben Lomond, California: Conciliar Press, 1999), p 33.
[4]   Timothy Ware, *The Orthodox Church* (London: Penguin Books, 1969), p 271.
[5]   Harper, *A Faith Fulfilled*, p 99.

deification has a unique role in this process, as through it deification of the whole creation would be achieved. Lossky describes this link between deification of man and creation: 'Finally, the cosmic Adam, by giving himself without return to God, would give Him back all His creation ... Thus in the overcoming of the primordial separation of the created and uncreated, there would be accomplished man's deification, and by him, of the whole universe.'[6]

Thirdly, this paper will present a view of deification and union with Christ as largely accepted by Orthodox and Reformed theologians respectively. The doctrine of deification has been developing throughout the centuries.[7] Fairbairn makes a particularly significant distinction between the two strands of deification among the Eastern Fathers.[8] On the one hand, Irenaeus, Athanasius and Cyril of Alexandria speak of deification primarily in personal terms. In this view salvation is first of all personal communion with the Triune God. Alongside this dominant emphasis they also speak of salvation as sharing in God's incorruption.[9]

On the other hand, there is a strand which primarily sees salvation as overcoming human mortality and corruption and so the centre of attention is on sharing in God's characteristic. This strand

---

[6] Vladimir Lossky, *Orthodox Theology: An Introduction* (trans. Ian and Ihita Kesarcodi-Watson; Crestwood, New York: St. Vladimir's Seminary Press, 1978), p 74.

[7] For a recent detailed survey of the patristic doctrine of deification see Norman Russell, *The Doctrine of Deification in the Greek Patristic Tradition* (The Oxford Early Christian Studies; Oxford: University Press, 2004).

[8] Regarding salvation Fairbairn recognises three strands among Church fathers: 'mystical,' 'personal,' and 'juridical.' He points out that this division is deliberately oversimplified: "Much more commonly, patristic theologians combined elements of two or even all three of them. This is certainly true, but I suggest that in most cases, one or another of these predominated, and therefore the use of this schema is helpful even though it is admittedly oversimplified." He further says: "I suggest that the Western Church fathers did lean noticeably (but not exclusively) toward the juridical pattern, and that Eastern theologians tended toward either the mystical or the personal pattern."—Donald Fairbairn, *Patristic Soteriology: Three Trajectories, JETS* 50/2 (June 2007): p 294.

[9] Fairbairn, *Patristic Soteriology,* p 304.

also speaks of salvation in personal terms but the focus is 'on participation in what later Eastern theology calls God's "energies."'[10]

Describing the development of this strand, Fairbairn writes:

> The emphases of Origen and Gregory of Nyssa were echoed prominently in the writings of Pseudo-Dionysius early in the sixth century. Later, Maximus the Confessor (ca. 580–662) launched an extensive critique of Origen's cosmology, allegedly solving once-for-all the problems inherent in it, but in my opinion he did not significantly depart from the overall vision of Origen and Gregory of Nyssa. This trajectory may be traced further through Gregory Palamas (ca. 1269–1359), who crystallized the distinction between God's essence (in which we do not share) and his energies (in which we do share through salvation). With Palamas the Eastern Orthodox Church was locked onto a trajectory in which salvation consists more of participation in God's qualities, his energies, rather than participation in a relationship.[11]

Since this second strand has had dominant influence on modern Orthodox thought, the doctrine of deification will be presented in accordance with this strand.[12]   In doing so, rather than directly citing

---

[10]   Fairbairn, *Patristic Soteriology*, p 304.

[11]   Fairbairn, *Patristic Soteriology*, p 308.

[12]   It must nevertheless be acknowledged that the first strand has more similarities with the doctrine of union with Christ than the second strand, particularly concerning the way that salvation is obtained. Regarding salvation, following Harnack's remarks that in the Early Church there were two views on sin and salvation, Fairbairn labels them as a three-act and a two-act of salvation. He further says: "The three-act scheme sees humanity as created (the first act) in a state of immortality and fellowship with God and views the fall (the second act) as a radical departure from the good condition in which God had originally placed Adam and Eve. Salvation (the third act) is understood primarily as a restoration of people to the original condition of perfect fellowship ... In contrast, the two-act view sees humanity's original created state (the first act) more as one of opportunity than as one of perfection ... This view places less emphases on the fall than a three-act scheme does, and it sees redemption (the second act) as the work of the incarnate Christ in leading humanity to a higher level, assisting

the Church fathers, they will be quoted as they are used by modern Orthodox theologians.

The doctrine of union with Christ was developed by Calvin, but since then it has undergone various shifts in emphases and formulations.[13] Particularly, Reformed theologians have been considering the relationship between different elements in the process of the application of salvation (which has been known as the *ordo salutis* – the order of salvation[14]) to one another and to union with Christ.

However, I intend to present a view which is in accordance with Calvin's view, where justification and sanctification are inseparable and both grounded in union with Christ. Furthermore, in taking this view as largely accepted by Reformed theologians I lean on Gaffin, who makes the connection between post-Reformation developments of the position of union with Christ in the *ordo salutis* and the Westminster Standards. He says: 'Perhaps better than any other documents, they provide us with a window on what has proven to be settled consensus down to the present of Reformed thinking on the matters they address.'[15] After brief analysis of what the Larger (Question and Answer 58-90) and Shorter (Question and Answer 29-

---

people in fulfilling their vocation, rather than as a restoration to a previous condition." Fairbairn further shows that both Athanasius and Cyril of Alexandria hold a three-act scheme of salvation.—Donald Fairbairn, *Grace and Christology in the Early Church* (Oxford Early Christian Studies; Oxford: University Press, 2003), pp 17-18 and pp 64-69. As this paper will show, Calvin's doctrine of union with Christ could be placed in a three-act scheme of salvation while the second strand of deification is a two-act scheme of salvation.

[13] William B. Evans, *Imputation and Impartation: Union with Christ in American Reformed Tradition* (Studies in Christian History and Thought; Milton Keynes: Paternoster, 2008) offers a very useful overview of the historical developments of the doctrine.

[14] The list of events in which God applies salvation to us personally is: election, the gospel call, regeneration, conversion, justification, adoption, sanctification, perseverance, death, glorification.—See, e.g. Wayne Grudem, *Systematic Theology: an introduction to Biblical Doctrine* (Leicester: IVP, 1994), p 841.

[15] Gaffin, "Union with Christ," pp 280-281.

32) Catechism say on this topic, Gaffin concludes that the Westminster Standards have 'essentially Calvin's *ordo salutis*, though not as clearly expressed as it could be.'[16]

Therefore, although there are different views from Calvin's position on union with Christ among Reformed thinkers, given that my aim is to compare salvation in Orthodoxy and Reformed thinking *in general*, I will not be considering these variations.

---

[16]   Gaffin, "Union with Christ," pp 281-282.

1. The Eastern Orthodox doctrine of Deification

1.1. *The Function of Deification*

Deification in Eastern Orthodoxy describes humanity's ultimate calling to be like God, found in the Scriptures. According to Stavropoulos, Psalm 82:6 (and John 10:34 which quotes Psalm 82:6) expresses this calling: 'I said: "You are gods, sons of the Most High, all of you."' The Apostle Peter (2 Peter 1:4) further explains the purpose of life. We are to 'become partakers of the divine nature.'[17]

These two verses are the Orthodox biblical foundation of the concept of deification. In addition, the gospel of John and Paul's letters use the language of mutual indwelling of God and men and of their personal union, and according to Ware so refer to the Orthodox doctrine of deification and prove that it is 'far from being unscriptural.'[18]

The term "deification" comes from the Greek "*theosis*," and means "the state of being god."[19] The term was expressed first by Irenaeus and later by Athanasius with regards to the Incarnation: "God became man so that men might become gods."[20] These words were repeated by the Fathers and Orthodox theologians in every century with the same emphasis: 'a descent of God which opens to

---

[17]   Christoforos Stavropoulos, *Partakers of Divine Nature* (trans. Stanley Harakas; Minneapolis, Minn.: Light and Life, 1976), p 17-18.

[18]   Ware, *The Orthodox Church* pp 220-21.

[19]   Stephen Thomas, *Deification in the Eastern Orthodox Tradition: A Biblical Perspective* (Piscataway, New Jersey: Gorgias Press, 2007), p 7.

[20]   Irenaeus writes; "If the Word is made man it is that men might become gods."— Irenaeus, *Against Heresies* 5, preface. Cited by Vladimir Lossky, *The Vision of God* (Crestwood, New York: St. Vladimir's Seminary Press, 1983), p 42. Athanasius says: "He, indeed, assumed humanity that we might become God."— St Athanasius, *On the Incarnation* (trans. A Religious of CSMV; Rev. ed.; New York: St Vladimir's Seminary Press, 1993), p 93

man a path of ascent.'[21]

The concept of "becoming god" is a broad one. According to Clendenin when the Greek Fathers refer to it in the *Philokalia*, a collection of Orthodox writings, they use a number of different words, such as union, transformation, partaking, participation, interpenetration, adoption and commingling.[22] Thus in order to understand the concept of deification, we will consider three interrelated aspects of this process. These aspects are: communion with God, becoming immortal and incorruptible, and growing into the likeness of God.[23]

Firstly, deification denotes communion with God. The deified person is in union with Christ's humanity, and through it, shares in the fellowship of the Trinity. Communion with God indicates that one is a child of God. According to Stavropoulos; 'The meaning of *Theosis* in the New Testament is the adoption of man.'[24] In this union the distinction between the Creator and the creature is not breached. Ware rejects all forms of pantheism and says that when we "become god" we do not lose our free will nor do we cease to be human.[25] Lossky explains that partaking in the divine nature means to be in union with God in his *energies*:

> The union to which we are called is neither hypostatic—as in the case of the human nature of Christ—nor substantial, as in the case of the three divine Persons: it is union with God in His energies, or union by grace making us participate in the divine nature, without our essence becoming thereby the

---

[21]   Vladimir Lossky, *In the Image and Likeness of God* (Oxford: Mowbray, 1975), p 97.
[22]   Daniel B. Clendenin, *Eastern Orthodox Christianity: A Western Perspective* (Grand Rapids: Baker, 1994), p 131.
[23]   Donald Fairbairn, *Eastern Orthodoxy through Western Eyes* (Louisville, Kentucky: Westminster John Knox Press, 2002), 71-2; or Clendenin, *Eastern Orthodox Christianity*, pp 131-34 and p 157.
[24]   Stavropoulos, *Partakers of Divine Nature*, pp 24-25.
[25]   Ware, *Orthodox Church*, p 237.

essence of God.[26]

The essential point for the understanding of union with God in Orthodoxy is therefore related to the distinction between God's essence and his energies. According to Thomas, 'the grace of God is an uncreated active power or energy. This energy is 'attached to its source,' that is, to the divine nature.'[27] He further says that energies refer to 'God's action in space and time by which he makes himself present to humankind.'[28] Similarly, Lossky writes:

> In the tradition of the Eastern Church grace usually signifies all the abundance of the divine nature, in so far as it is communicated to men; the deity which operates outside the essence and gives itself, the divine nature of which we partake through the uncreated energies.[29]

We can thus understand the energies of God as the activity of God as opposed to his essence. The energies serve as a bridge between the divine and human nature.[30] Human participation in the divine life is so not union with his essence, but union with his energies. Through this union people are deified and in this life union 'can be made more and more real.'[31] The fullness of union will be realised fully after the resurrection from the dead.[32]

Secondly, deification can be understood as obtaining immortality and incorruptibility. This view of salvation as escape from death and corruption, as expounded by the Greek Fathers,

---

[26] Vladimir Lossky, *The Mystical Theology of the Eastern Church* (London: James Clarke and Co. Ltd, 1957), p 70.

[27] Thomas, *Deification*, p 25.

[28] Thomas, *Deification*, p 33.

[29] Lossky, *Mystical Theology*, pp 162-163.

[30] Panayiotis Nellas, *Deification in Christ: Orthodox Perspectives on the Nature of the Human Person* (trans. Norman Russell; Crestwood, New York: St Vladimir's Seminary Press, 1987), p 32.

[31] Stavropoulos, *Partakers of Divine Nature*, p 30.

[32] Georgios I. Mantzaridis, *The Deification of Man: St. Gregory Palamas and the Orthodox Tradition* (trans. Liadain Sherrard; Crestwood, New York: St. Vladimir's Seminary Press, 1984), p 117.

stems from the Eastern Orthodox understanding of the consequences of sin. For example, Athanasius sees death and corruption as a penalty for transgression of God's command.[33] In the process of deification, as we participate in the divine life, we receive immortality and incorruptibility which are natural to God. In this way 'the elevation of the human being to the divine sphere' happens. However, this elevation does not mean that our essence is transformed into that of God; rather, it is 'the union of the whole person with God as unrestricted happiness in the divine kingdom.'[34]

The third aspect of deification is the transformation from the image to the likeness of God. The image of God is the common property of all men and signifies the realised state given at the moment of creation.[35] Likeness conveys 'something dynamic and not yet realized.'[36] It is realisation of our potential to be similar to God, manifested in our lives primarily by love, God's leading characteristic.[37] Despite sin, the image of God cannot be lost, while likeness depends on man's moral choice and is under the influence of sin, which destroys it.[38] Thus, the likeness of God is both the process and the final phase of deification. Through our participation in the divine life, we become more godlike, we are transformed in the likeness of the Christ, the perfect image of the Father.[39]

Accordingly, the relationship between man and God in the Eastern Orthodox tradition is a dynamic relationship, since we are created to grow and achieve the likeness of God. Man's state before

---

[33] St Athanasius, *On the Incarnation*, pp 29-30.

[34] Stavropoulos, *Partakers of Divine Nature*, p 18.

[35] Referring to the image of God in Orthodoxy, Ware says that "the west has often associated the image of God with man's intellect. While many Orthodox have done the same, others would say that since man is a single unified whole, the image of God embraces his entire person, body as well as soul."—Ware, *Orthodox Church*, p 225.

[36] Mantzaridis, *The Deification of Man*, p 21.

[37] Thomas, *Deification in the Eastern Orthodox Tradition*, p 29.

[38] Ware, *Orthodox Church*, p 224.

[39] Lossky, *The Vision of God*, p 98.

the fall was a state of 'an unstable perfection in which the fullness of union is not yet achieved and in which created beings have still to grow in love in order to accomplish fully the thought-will of God.'[40] Following Irenaeus, Ware describes this state as a state of innocence and simplicity.[41] Thus, man was created as immature, and set upon the road to complete union, with the goals of achieving fellowship with God and growing increasingly into his likeness.

1.2. The Content of Deification

1.2.1. The role of Jesus Christ

According to Orthodox understanding, due to his sin Adam did not fulfil his vocation to raise himself up to God. Nonetheless, humanity's calling after the fall remained the same: to know union with God. But this goal was impossible because of sin, death, and the chasm between the human and divine nature.[42] It was therefore necessary that God would descend to man. Through Christ the obstacles to the ultimate vocation of mankind were removed. By his death on the cross Jesus destroyed sin and by his resurrection he triumphed over death. The distance between the human and divine natures was abolished by Jesus' birth, as the Son of God united to himself a human nature.

Thus the main goal of the Incarnation in Eastern Orthodoxy is bridging the gap between the divine and human natures. With the Incarnation, the first human nature is grafted in to the divine life, and 'hence to all creatures the way to communion with this Life is open.'[43] As Christ's human nature was deified through it's hypostatic union with the Logos of God, it became 'able to comprehend the fullness of uncreated energy, it became an inexhaustible source,

---

[40] Lossky, *Mystical Theology*, p 97.
[41] Ware, *Orthodox Church*, p 225.
[42] Nellas, *Deification in Christ*, p 111.
[43] Georges Florovsky, *Creation and Redemption* (vol. 3 of *Collected Works*, Belmont, Mass.: Nordland, 1976), p 75.

transmitting this divinizing energy to men and thereby deifying them.'[44] Thus, Christ's body becomes the point of contact with God which opens the possibility of the fulfilment of mankind's calling to achieve deification. Consequently, the most important aspect of redemption for Orthodoxy is the Incarnation. In other words, since in Jesus the gap between the divine and human nature is overcome, the focus is on the person of Jesus Christ, that is, on *who he is*.

1.2.2.   *The role of the Holy Spirit*

Deification is the result of the Holy Spirit's work in people. The indispensable work of Christ is complemented by the work of the Holy Spirit. Lossky describes it; 'The Son has become like us by the incarnation; we become like Him by deification, by partaking of the divinity in the Holy Spirit, who communicates the divinity to *each* human person in a particular way.'[45] Similarly, Stavropoulos explains that our union with God is offered by Christ's work and realised only in the Holy Spirit: 'Only in the Holy Spirit will we reach the point of becoming gods, the likeness of God.'[46] By the grace of the Holy Spirit, that is, by his sanctifying uncreated energy in us, God affects our spiritual life and transforms us into the divine likeness.[47] The Holy Spirit's 'sanctifying and deifying energy is actualized in the holy services of the church, especially in holy baptism, repentance, and the divine Eucharist.'[48]

1.2.3.   *The role of the Church*

Deification takes place in the context of Christ's body, the Church. Eastern Orthodoxy sees the Church as the body of Christ and the fullness of life in the Holy Spirit. Lossky writes about her nature; 'The

---

[44]   Mantzaridis, *The Deification of Man*, p 33.

[45]   Lossky, *In the Image and Likeness of God*, p 109.

[46]   Stavropoulos, *Partakers of Divine Nature*, p 29.

[47]   Emil Bartos, *Deification in Eastern Orthodox theology: An Evaluation and Critique of the Theology of Dumitru Staniloae* (Carlisle: Paternoster, 1999), p 290.

[48]   Stavropoulos, *Partakers of Divine Nature*, p 192.

Church is *body* in so far as Christ is her head; she is *fullness* in so far as the Holy Spirit quickens her and fills her with divinity, for the Godhead dwells within her bodily as it dwelt in the deified humanity of Christ.'[49] The Church itself constitutes the place where salvation becomes concrete, where 'the spiritual life of the Head flows down to the members and gives them life,'[50] and as such, the Church is a necessary channel of salvation.

Through the sacraments of the Church, the power of the Holy Spirit is believed to complete the process of sanctification in believers.[51] Baptism and chrismation set a person on the road of deification. Baptism has a multiple function.[52] Baptism is 'literally a new birth in Christ and in this sense a new creation of man.' It regenerates the image of God in us and cleanses us from our personal sin. Thus, baptism is the beginning of union with Christ and through it man participates in Christ's death and resurrection. According to Palamas, through baptism man also becomes the son of God.[53] Chrismation follows immediately after Baptism and through it man receives the Holy Spirit and his gifts.

After this beginning of life in union with God, the Eucharist is the supreme means through which deification takes place. In the Eucharist 'the faithful truly participate in the real body and blood of Christ... [and] they receive the divine life and deification.'[54] That is, the bread and wine are not mere symbols but they become the body and blood of Christ.[55] The flesh of the Lord, then, through hypostatic union is passed to those who receive bread and wine and the divine

---

[49] Lossky, *Mystical Theology,* p 157.
[50] Nellas, *Deification in Christ,* p 113.
[51] Karmaris, John. "Concerning the Sacraments." in *Eastern Orthodox Theology: A Contemporary Reader.* 2d ed. Edited by Daniel B. Clendenin. (Carlisle: Paternoster, 2003) p 22.
[52] See, e.g. Nellas, *Deification in Christ,* p 121 and p 124.
[53] Mantzaridis, *The Deification of Man,* p 48.
[54] Karmaris, "Concerning the Sacraments," pp 26-27.
[55] Ware, *Orthodox Church,* p 290.

life is transferred to them.[56] This leads to remission of sins of the faithful and further to immortality and eternal life.[57] Thus, through the Eucharist, 'our human nature is intertwined with Christ, intermingled with the Divine reality and is divinized,' and so we become gods.[58]

1.2.4. *The role of human work*

In addition to the sacraments, the Holy Spirit also works through human effort, which makes man capable of receiving deification.[59] Prayer, fasting and other works, as Stavropoulos explains, are 'necessary means for the achievement of the purpose' of the receiving of the Holy Spirit.[60] As we make the Holy Spirit our own, we in turn are deified by his grace. That is, as we freely cooperate with God and grow in virtue the divine grace is able to increase within us.[61] Thus, to achieve full fellowship with God, alongside the divine grace, virtue is equally a necessary force.[62] Lossky sums up well the relation between human responsibility and deification; 'God becomes *powerless* before human freedom... Certainly man was created by the will of God alone; but he cannot be deified by it alone.'[63]

1.2.5. *Salvation as a process*

Deification begins with baptism and chrismation. From this point man is on 'a difficult and long journey,'[64] which leads to full union with God. On this way of ascent, through faith, the Eucharist, good work and constant repentance, man cooperates with the divine grace and is deified.

---

[56] Karmaris, "Concerning the Sacraments," p 26.
[57] Karmaris, "Concerning the Sacraments," p 26.
[58] Stavropoulos, *Partakers of Divine Nature*, p 60.
[59] Mantzaridis, *The Deification of Man*, p 88.
[60] Stavropoulos, *Partakers of Divine Nature*, p 33.
[61] Stavropoulos, *Partakers of Divine Nature*, p 35.
[62] Ware, *Orthodox Church*, pp 226-27.
[63] Lossky, *Orthodox Theology*, p 73.
[64] Stavropoulos, *Partakers of Divine Nature*, p 49.

The process of deification will be completed only after the resurrection of the dead, as even after man's death further transformation is possible through the prayers of believers. In Orthodoxy those who pray for man's deification are both the present and past generations of believers. Zernov explains this: 'The Orthodox do not regard the saints as mediators, but as teachers and friends who pray with them and assist them in their spiritual ascent.' In the process of deification, 'the saints are those who, having advanced nearer to the ultimate goal, can uplift the rest.'[65]

This further improvement in deification is viable because the believer will be rewarded only after the resurrection of the dead, when the process of deification will be completed. Zernov again writes:

> The final reckoning can be made only at the end of history. So even the blessed do not reach their full glory immediately after death and those who failed to learn how to love in freedom are not deprived of improvement in their position through the compassion of their friends. So the Orthodox Church prays for all the departed, both saints and sinners, trusting in the power of mutual love and forgiveness.[66]

Deification thus finally ends after the resurrection of the dead, when it becomes perfect and irreversible.[67]

---

[65] Nicolas Zernov, *Eastern Christendom: A Study of the Origin and Development of the Eastern Orthodox Church*, (Readers Union ed.; London: Weidenfeld and Nicolson, 1963), p 233.

[66] Zernov, *Eastern Christendom*, p 235.

[67] Mantzaridis, *The Deification of Man*, p 117.

2. The Reformed doctrine of Union with Christ

2.1. The Function of Union with Christ

Union with Christ has a central place in every aspect of salvation in the Reformed tradition. Turretin points to this foundational place of union; 'from union with Christ depends the communion of all his benefits.' [68] That is, those united to Christ receive the blessings of justification, adoption, sanctification and glorification. The phrase "union with Christ" refers to the mutual indwelling of Christ and believers. Although the phrase does not occur in the Bible, this union is expressed by the phrase "in Christ" or "in the Lord," found most frequently in Paul's letters but also elsewhere (e.g. John 15:4-7; 1 John 2:28). [69]

The nature of union with Christ is spiritual, as the bond of this union is the Holy Spirit. [70] Romans 8:9-10 describes the relationship between Christ, the Holy Spirit and believers:

> You however, are controlled not by the sinful nature but by the Spirit, if the Spirit of God lives in you. And if anyone does not have the Spirit of Christ, he does not belong to Christ. But if Christ is in you, your body is dead because of sin, yet your spirit is alive because of righteousness.

The Spirit of God dwells in believers, he is the "Spirit of Christ," and Christ is in believers. Consequently, if the Spirit dwells in believers, it is Christ who dwells in them by the Spirit. This in turn means that a person united to Christ's humanity participates in the life of the

---

[68] Francis Turretin, *Institutes of Elenctic Theology* (vol 2. ed. James T. Dennison; trans. George Musgrave Giger; Phillipsburg, New Jersey: P&R, 1994), p 668.

[69] John 17 has an important place in considering union with Christ in Reformed tradition.

[70] See, e.g. John Murray, *Redemption Accomplished and Applied* (London: The Banner of Truth Trust, 1961), p 166.

Trinity. Jesus says to his Father in John 17:21; 'just as you are in me and I am in you.' Thus those who are united with Jesus have communion with the three distinct persons of the Godhead, Father, Son and Holy Spirit.

Union with Christ is thus personal and it has a filial facet, God is our Father (Romans 8:15). The intimacy of this union is depicted by its comparison to the relationship between husband and wife (Ephesians 5:32). Galatians 2:20 points out that this union is essential for the Christian life: 'I no longer live, but Christ lives in me.' However, since it is spiritual in nature, union with Christ preserves the distinction of united persons. Gaffin explains that the union is neither like the union between Father, Son and Holy Spirit, nor like that of Christ's two natures, nor like between body and soul, nor like between husband and wife. Neither is this union merely intellectual and moral.[71] Rather, union in Christ denotes a spiritual relationship, where distinction between the divine and human nature is maintained.

The extent of union with Christ is as Murray writes, 'a very broad and embracive subject.'[72] Every aspect of the relationship between God and believer is in some way related to this union.[73] Accordingly, every aspect of salvation is received in Christ (Ephesians 1:3). Thus, union with Christ can be considered from three different aspects. These aspects are: election in Christ, sharing in Christ's work and personal application of the blessings achieved by Christ.

Firstly, union with Christ precedes the creation of the world, when God the Father chose the elect in Christ.[74] Ephesians 1:4-5 says: 'For he chose us in him, before the creation of the world to be holy and blameless in his sight. In love he predestined us to be adopted as his sons through Jesus Christ, in accordance with his pleasure and will.' When the Father elected man from eternity to be saved, he

---

[71] Gaffin, "Union with Christ," p 274.
[72] Murray, *Redemption*, p 169.
[73] Grudem, *Systematic Theology*, p 840.
[74] Ephesians 1:4; 2 Timothy 1:9.

thought about them as being "in Christ" even though they did not yet exist.[75] This means that God did not choose the elect first, and then decide to bring the elect into union with Christ. Rather, salvation is received in Christ, including election. Eternal election therefore cannot be separated from union with Christ.[76] However, it is important to note at this point that eternal election neither denies that man is born as spiritually dead, under the wrath of God and in need of repentance and conversion; nor does it mean that a Christian life of holiness is unnecessary.

Secondly, union with Christ refers to the union which man has in Christ's death and resurrection. Through union with Christ, the people of God share in his death on the cross (e.g. Romans 6:3-11). That is, Jesus' death on the cross was in our place. Believers also share in Christ's resurrection and exaltation to heaven, as God 'raised us up with him and seated us with him in the heavenly places in Christ Jesus' (Ephesians 2:6). This means that Jesus' resurrection was for us. Romans 4:25 brings Jesus' death and resurrection for us together in one verse: 'He was delivered over to death *for our sins* and was raised to life *for our justification.*'[77] Letham writes: 'We died and rose in him [Jesus] because he was our representative. We died and rose in him because his death and resurrection have dynamic power by the Holy Spirit, transforming us and raising us to new life. We died and rose in him because of the intimate personal union that prevails.'[78]

Thus, from these two aspects of union of with Christ, we see that this union is rooted in God's election before the foundation of the world and so it has no beginning. It leads to the future glorification of the believers and so also has no end.[79]

---

[75] Grudem, *Systematic Theology*, p 841.
[76] Robert Letham, *The Work of Christ* (Contours of Christian Theology; Downers Grove, Ill.: IVP, 1993), p 86.
[77] Italics mine.
[78] Letham, *The Work of Christ*, p 85.
[79] Murray, *Redemption*, p 162 and p 164.

The third aspect of union with Christ is the actual application of salvation, through which the believer has a personal relationship with God and receives all the benefits of Christ's work. The actual application of Christ's work comes by the work of the Holy Spirit and through faith in Jesus Christ, and it will be considered in more detail in the next section. It is significant however, as Gaffin observes, to notice these different aspects of union with Christ, and to recognise which aspect brings to the believer the actual enjoyment of its benefits. He further says: 'At the same time, it is no less important to maintain each of them and to do so without equivocating on them, either by denying any one of them or blurring the distinction between them.'[80]

2.2. The Content of Union with Christ

2.2.1. The role of Jesus Christ

When Adam disobeyed God, the relationship between humans and God was broken. The result of sin, according to the Reformed tradition, is so severe that man is unable on his own to obtain the fellowship with God which he enjoyed before the fall, due to spiritual death. Ephesians 2:1-3 pictures this present state of humanity, describing people as dead in their trespasses and sins and as the sons of disobedience. Sin also made us to be enemies of God (Romans 5:10), put us under his wrath (1 Thessalonians 1:10) and brought us under God's penalty and judgement (2 Thessalonians 1:8-10).

The incarnation, therefore, was necessary for man's salvation since only a human being, another Adam, could atone for the human sin of the first Adam and undo its consequences.[81] Through Christ's death on the cross and his resurrection, God saves people from death and the bondage of sin, and at the same time remains faithful to his promise to punish sin (Genesis 3:15).

---

[80] Gaffin, "Union with Christ," p 275.
[81] Letham, *The Work of Christ*, p 78.

Furthermore, two important things stem from Jesus' death on the cross. Firstly, Jesus bore *the punishment* for our sin when he died. God has laid on Jesus the iniquity of us all (Isaiah 53:6) and he himself bore our sins in his body on the cross (1 Peter 2:24). Secondly, Jesus bore the punishment for our sin *instead of us*, as a substitute. Christ died for us (Romans 5:8) and he 'redeemed us from the curse of the law by becoming a curse for us' (Galatians 3:13). Accordingly, the most important aspect of redemption in Reformed tradition is the work of Christ on the cross. The focus is on what *he has done* for us.

2.2.2. *The role of the Holy Spirit*

The work of Jesus Christ has no value for man until the Holy Spirit applies it to him personally. Unless we are united to Christ, we can neither enjoy the aspect of union related to election nor can we have any benefit of union based on Christ's death and resurrection. Calvin says that 'we must understand that as long as Christ remains outside of us, and we are separated from him, all that he has suffered and done for the salvation of the human race remains useless and of no value for us.'[82]

As humanity cannot deal with sin on its own and is in the state of death and corruption, separated from God and unable to trust him, the Spirit's regenerating work is necessary.[83] The Holy Spirit makes those who are chosen spiritually alive, convicts them of their sin, enlightens them to the sufficiency of the work of Christ on the cross, and makes them willing and able to receive Jesus as their Saviour and Lord. [84] As such, the work of the Holy Spirit is irresistible and sovereign (John 3:8). This further means that faith is a result of

---

[82] John Calvin, *Institutes of the Christian Religion* (ed. John T. McNeill; trans. Ford Lewis Battles; 2 vols; LCC 20-21; Philadelphia: Westminster, 1960), III.i.1 (1:537), III.i.4 (Battles 1:537).

[83] The Holy Spirit is also the agent of sanctification which will be considered under section 2.2.4 below.

[84] Reymond, *New Systematic Theology*, p 718.

his work and a gift from God. Thus, the Holy Spirit has an essential role in the whole process of the application of salvation.

2.2.3. *The role of faith*

Union with Christ on the personal level comes into reality through faith, that is, through trusting Jesus for salvation. Faith, as God's gift, is related to the regenerative work of the Holy Spirit. Regeneration is in turn inseparable from God's election and his call (Romans 8:30— those whom God predestined he also called (as well as justified and glorified)).

The calling is an act of God the Father (Romans 8:29). Reformed theology distinguishes between God's general and effective call. God's general call is the call to all people to repent and believe the gospel. Through the effective call God summons his chosen people to himself (John 6:44), that is, God achieves his eternal purpose and applies salvation to chosen people. God's call comes through the proclamation of the gospel, and so faith is linked to hearing God's word (Romans 10:14). The beginning of union with Christ through faith is thus inseparable not just from regeneration but also from repentance. Repentance, in the same manner as faith, is God's gift.[85]

2.2.4. *Blessings received through union with Christ personally applied*

o   *Justification*

Justification takes place when a person is united to Christ by faith. The term justification in the Bible refers to God's act by which a sinner is put in a right relation to God, as his sins are forgiven and he is accepted and treated as righteous. As such, justification refers to a new status of the believer before God: the believer once was under God's wrath but now is without guilt, reconciled to him and at peace with him (Romans 5:1, 10).

---

[85]   Cf. Acts 11:18—Letham, *The Work of Christ*, p 81.

The basis of justification is union with Christ, through which the believer's guilt is transferred to Christ, and Christ's righteousness is transferred to the believer. 2 Corinthians 5:21 describes this: 'God made him who had no sin to be sin for us, so that in him we might become the righteousness of God.' Calvin describes the relationship between justification and union with Christ and explains that Christ's righteousness is imputed to us. He first says that 'indwelling of Christ in our hearts ... that mystical union' is of the highest importance for Christians as through it they share in his gifts. He then proceeds as follows:

> We do not, therefore, contemplate him outside ourselves from afar in order that his righteousness may be imputed to us, but because we put on Christ and are engrafted into his body - in short, because he deigns to make us one with him. For this reason, we glory that we have fellowship of righteousness with him.[86]

Thus for Calvin, an imputed righteousness is realised in union with Christ. As such, an imputed righteousness is not possible apart from union with Christ because 'it is not an abstract entity but *his* righteousness that is imputed to me, reckoned as mine.'[87]

Furthermore, there is neither imputation of Christ's righteousness without union, nor is there union without imputation. However, the basis for the believer's righteousness is not in that union. Rather, that basis comes from Christ's own righteousness. His righteousness was 'established and completed in his obedience culminating in his death, which, in union in him, is imputed to me. Just as it is *his*, as distinct from any righteousness I might manifest, it is reckoned as *mine*.'[88]

---

[86] Calvin, *Inst.* III.xi.10 (1:737).
[87] Gaffin, "Union with Christ," p 286.
[88] Gaffin, "Union with Christ," pp 286-287.

o *Adoption*

Adoption stands in relation to union with Christ as 'an effect to its cause.'[89] That is, being united to Christ, we are adopted into God's family and we become the children of God (John 1:12; Galatians 4:4-6). Adoption is, like justification, an act of God and a bestowal of a status.[90] Just as we are clothed with Jesus' righteousness, we are clothed with his relationship to the Father, and so through him we participate in sonship.[91] As the sons and daughters of God, we have a personal relationship and communion with God whom we know and approach as our Father.

o *Sanctification*

Sanctification is also an outcome of union with Christ. It refers to a life of holiness (Romans 6:1-14), 'without which no one will see the Lord' (Hebrews 12:14).   As Calvin explains, justification does not abolish our need for holiness and good works. Rather, sanctification is inseparable from justification because of the nature of our union with Christ and because he 'contains both of them inseparable in himself.'[92] Calvin illustrates this by using the Sun and its light and heat as a metaphor.[93] Describing Calvin's view, Gaffin writes:

> Christ, our righteousness, is the Sun, justification, its light, sanctification, its heat. The Sun is at once the source of both, so that light and heat are inseparable. But only light illumines and only heat warms, not the reverse. Both are always present, without the one becoming the other.[94]

Sanctification involves our inner transformation (2 Corinthians 3:18). It is a life-long process which leads to conformation to the image of

---

[89]   Turretin, *Institutes of Elenctic Theology*, p 669.
[90]   Murray, *Redemption*, p 133.
[91]   Mike Ovey, *Application of the Cross Work* (3), (Unpublished papers, Oak Hill College, 2007).
[92]   Calvin, *Inst.* III.xvi.1 (1:798).
[93]   Calvin *Inst.* III.xi.6 (1:732).
[94]   Gaffin, "Union with Christ", p 284.

Jesus Christ (Romans 8:29-30). The agent of sanctification is the Holy Spirit who dwells and works in believers. Human effort is also necessary in achieving holiness. This work is not the basis for our acceptance and salvation; rather it is living a life of pleasing God. As such, our work stems from the gratitude to God for salvation and is a response to his work in us.[95]

o   *Glorification*

Glorification of believers is an outcome of union with Christ. Those whom God has chosen and called to believe in Christ will persevere to the end because of the sovereign work of God, that is because they 'are being guarded through faith for a salvation ready to be revealed in the last time' by God's power (I Peter 1:5).

However, having said that believers will persevere because of the sovereign activity of God, it is important to say that preservation of believers by God does not deny the need for human active response. Believers are to use all the means ordained by God in order to persevere (e.g. reading God's word and fellowship with other Christians) and remain in faith and holiness until the end.[96] This human involvement is not work necessary for salvation. This work, as I Peter 1:5 says, is through *faith* which is grounded in God's power and electing grace. Commenting on verses 21 and 24-25 in Jude, Berkouwer explains this:

> We will never be able to understand these words if we see the divine preservation and our preservation of ourselves as mutually exclusive or as in a synthetic cooperation ... God's preservation and our self-preservation do not stand in mere coordination, but in a marvellous way they *are* in correlation. One can formulate it best in this way: *our* preservation of

---

[95]   Murray, *Redemption,* pp 148-49.
[96]   Murray, *Redemption,* pp 154-56.

ourselves is entirely oriented to *God's* preservation of us.[97]

Thus, those who are elected will persevere and be changed at the time of Christ's coming (1 Corinthians 15:51-52), and so be glorified, sharing in Christ's glory and being together with him.

2.2.5. *Salvation as status*

Union with Christ begins by faith in him. From that point man is adopted into God's family and made acceptable before God because of Christ's righteousness. This in turn is a guarantee that glorification will take place at Christ's second return. In the meantime, the Holy Spirit continues to sanctify and change the believer into the image of Christ.

---

[97] G. C. Berkouwer, *Faith and Perseverance* (Studies in Dogmatics; trans. R. D. Knudsen; Grand Rapids: Eerdmans, 1958), p 104.

3.   Evaluation and comparison

3.1.   Image and likeness

Since deification is the movement from the image to the likeness of God, deification is based on the distinction between the image and the likeness of God.[98] Orthodox theologians lean heavily on the use of both words in Genesis 1:26 'Let us make man in our image, in our likeness.' However, both in Genesis 1:26-28 and in 5:1-3 it is hard to find evidence in support of this distinction. Firstly, there is nothing in Genesis 1:26 that necessarily introduces this distinction (although the Septuagint and Vulgate insert the conjunction *and*, there is no conjunction in the Hebrew).[99] Genesis 5:1 further confirms that the image and likeness are used as synonyms, as it says that 'when God created man, he made him in the likeness of God.' Thus, as both image and likeness were clearly given at creation, it is unconvincing that "likeness" must be acquired after creation.[100]

Furthermore, this distinction between the image and likeness corresponds to the Orthodox concept of creation of man in a state of immaturity, with the aim of man's growth to achieve the likeness of God. Fairbairn points out that such a concept of man raises the question of God's responsibility for sin and evil.[101] Indeed, if 'it is possible to see in the initial state of the created cosmos an *unstable* perfection in which the fullness of union is not yet achieved,'[102] then one might conclude that sin is also a result of God's act of creation. In

---

[98]   Reformed theology makes a distinction between the image of God applicable to all people (James 3:9) and the renewed image in Christ in those who believe (Colossians 3:10).—See, e.g. Robert Letham, *Through Western Eyes* (Fearn, Ross-shire: Mentor, 2007), pp 243-44.

[99]   A.A. Hoekema, *Created in God's Image* (Exeter: Paternoster, 1986), p 13.

[100]   Fairbairn, *Eastern Orthodoxy through Western Eyes*, p 120.

[101]   Fairbairn, *Eastern Orthodoxy through Western Eyes*, pp 121-22.

[102]   Lossky, *Mystical Theology*, p 97. Italics mine.

contrast, if man is created in mature fellowship with God (without denial of the possibility of growth), then man is fully responsible for his actions.

3.2. Consequences of sin on the beginning of union with Christ

Different concepts of man's state before the fall influence the view of man's state after the fall, and this in turn brings a disparity with regards to how union with Christ begins. Just as in Orthodoxy, Adam fell 'from a state of undeveloped simplicity,' which is a less exalted state than in Western theology, so the consequences of the fall are also less severe than in Reformed theology.[103] Meyendorff describes the link between sin and it's consequences as mortality rather than sinfulness:

> There is indeed a consensus in Greek patristic and Byzantine traditions in identifying the inheritance of the Fall as an inheritance essentially of mortality rather than of sinfulness, sinfulness being merely a consequence of mortality.[104]

Thus, Adam's sin made union between man and God impossible, and corruption and death came into the world. Sin has not, however, deprived man of his freedom. Orthodoxy thus rejects the doctrine of original sin and claims that man sins by imitation of Adam.

While discussing Romans 5:12 and defending this view, Meyendorff gives its literal translation: "*because* of death, all men have sinned." Thus, he concludes: 'It is this death [mortality or "corruption"] which makes sin inevitable'.[105] Moo notes that although such a translation is certainly plausible, this position fails to explain why it is that *everyone* chooses to sin. He further says: 'Surely there must be something inherent in 'being human' that causes everyone, without exception, to decide to worship idols rather than the true God

---

[103] Ware, *Orthodox Church*, p 228.
[104] John Meyendorff, *Byzantine Theology: Historical Trends and Doctrinal Themes* (Oxford: Mowbrays, 1975), p 145.
[105] Meyendorff, *Byzantine Theology*, pp 144-45.

(cf. [Romans] 1:22-23)."[106] Moo concludes that an explanation of this reason, according to Romans 5:12-21, lies in human solidarity in the sin of Adam.[107] Consequently, in Orthodoxy man is free to choose to follow God, while in Reformed theology man is bound by sin and can respond to God only after God's regenerative work.

3.3. Synergism

Salvation as deification clearly involves human work. For example Florovsky writes: 'God has freely willed a synergistic path of redemption in which man must spiritually participate.'[108] Stavropoulos explains the relationship between the human and divine will, saying that divine grace comes after man 'freely makes the decision from within for the good and for the Christian life.'[109] Human decision comes first, grace second.

In contrast, in the Reformed tradition God's grace always comes first. The Christian life begins by faith through the irresistible work of the Holy Spirit. Human work and the life of holiness are important afterwards in the process of sanctification. However, they are both the effect of God's continuous work in the believer. Thus, a life of holiness is not for the purpose of being accepted; rather it is in response to God having already made us his children and declared us righteous.

Synergism is therefore *a vital difference* in achieving man's salvation. Deification takes place through the cooperative work of man and God, while in the Reformed tradition, faith, union and

---

[106] Douglas S. Moo, *The Epistle to the Romans* (NICNT; Cambridge: Eerdmans, 1996), p 324.

[107] For Moo's fuller discussion on translation of Romans 5:12 and its meaning in the context see Moo, *Romans*, pp 316-29.

[108] Georges Florovsky, *The Byzantine Ascetic and Spiritual Fathers* (Vol 10 of *Collected Works*; trans. Raymond Miller; Vaduz, Germany: Büchervertriebsanstalt, 1987), p 31.—Cited in Fairbairn, *Eastern Orthodoxy through Western Eyes*, p 91.

[109] Stavropoulos, *Partakers of Divine Nature*, p 35.

salvation are solely achieved through God's action (monergism). As we shall see, synergism has enormous consequences on the concepts of justification and adoption.

3.4. Atonement

Athanasius' maxim; "God became man so that men might become gods," accepted and repeated by Orthodox theologians of every century, has led the Eastern church to view Christ's atoning death as far less significant than his incarnation and resurrection.

Meyendorff describes what the atonement means for Orthodoxy:

> In the East the cross is envisaged not so much as the punishment of the just one, which 'satisfies' a transcendent Justice requiring a retribution for man's sins. As Georges Florovsky rightly puts it: 'the death of the Cross was effective, not as a death of an Innocent One, but as the death of the Incarnate Lord.' The point was not to satisfy a legal requirement, but to vanquish the frightful cosmic reality of death, which held humanity under its usurped control and pushed it into the vicious circle of sin and corruption.[110]

The emphasis in the atonement is thus freedom from sin and death. Consequently, the focus of Orthodox soteriology is the Incarnation and resurrection of Jesus Christ, who opened the way to union with God and deification.

Nevertheless, since some Orthodox theologians speak about the atonement in legal or juridical categories,[111] some hold the opinion that Orthodoxy shares the Western perspective about Christ's substitutionary death. That is, that the difference between these

---

[110] Meyendorff, *Byzantine theology*, p 161.
[111] For example, Lossky says: 'Through dereliction, through accursedness, an innocent person assumes all sin, 'substitutes' Himself for those who are justly condemned and suffers death for them.'—Lossky, *Orthodox Theology*, p 110.

perspectives is only in emphasis.[112] Ware illustrates this when he says that although Orthodoxy is focused on "Christ the Victor" and the post-medieval west on "Christ the Victim", we must not push this contrast too far. He further says:

> Eastern writers, as well as western, have applied juridical and penal language to the Crucifixion; western writers, as well as eastern, have never ceased to think of Good Friday as a moment of victory.[113]

However, there is a certain reluctance in Orthodoxy towards the idea of satisfaction of divine justice on the cross. This unease comes because it is perceived that God's justice is satisfied at the expense of his love. Thus, for Thomas, love is God's leading characteristic.[114] He quotes St. Isaac the Syrian to contrast Anselm's view of the atonement: 'We cannot possibly say that God acts out of retribution, even though the Scriptures may on the surface propose this'. And then he explains that 'the Orthodox Church sees mercy as a greater quality than justice.'[115]

Similarly, Florovsky says that 'there could hardly be any retributive justice in the Passion and death of the Lord.' Nor is Christ's suffering 'to be explained by the idea of a substitutional satisfaction, the *satisfactio vicaria* of the scholastics.' Rather, he asks a rhetorical question: 'Does Justice really restrain Love and Mercy, and was the Crucifixion needed to disclose the pardoning love of God, otherwise precluded from manifesting itself by the restraint of vindicatory justice?'[116] Thus for Florovsky the cross is a symbol of God's love rather than satisfaction of divine justice, which is 'an abstract justice.'[117] This means that the atonement is the effect of

---

[112] For example, Clendenin, *Eastern Orthodox Christianity*, pp 123-124; Fairbairn, *Eastern Orthodoxy through Western Eyes*, pp 6-7.

[113] Timothy Ware, *The Orthodox Church* (London: Penguin Books, 1969), p 234.

[114] Thomas, *Deification in the Eastern Orthodox Tradition*, p 29.

[115] Thomas, *Deification in the Eastern Orthodox Tradition*, p 23.

[116] Florovsky, *Creation and Redemption*, p 102.

[117] Florovsky, *Creation and Redemption*, pp 103-104.

God's love.

Analysing the juridical aspect of the atonement in the theology of the two most important Russian theologians of the 20th century, Lossky and Florovsky, Richardson argues that 'they radically de-emphasise juridical categories, formally affirming their existence while practically all but denying their contribution to soteriology and that this, in particular, stems from a profound aversion towards the concept of divine retributive punishment."[118] This could be, in my opinion, extended to the Eastern Orthodox view in general. Therefore, rather than just being the issue of different emphases in the atonement, as being focused on sin and death in East and on satisfaction of divine justice in West, it is better to acknowledge that the juridical aspect of the atonement in Orthodoxy is neither central nor even secondary.

In Reformed theology, however, Christ is not just the one who heals our disease and who brought the victory over sin and death[119] (which is certainly less emphasised than in the East), but the one who became man in order to substitute himself for us and to pay our debt to satisfy divine justice and to appease God's wrath. Sin brings not just personal alienation from God and corruption, but it is also a personal transgression of the law for which man is held responsible. Since we were unable to repay our debt, it was necessary that Christ deal with our guilt (Galatians 2:21). His atoning death was also sufficient (Hebrews 10:11-14). Moreover, just as in Orthodoxy, his death is also the greatest proof of God's love (e.g. John 3:16; Romans 5:8). The atonement is thus equally the effect of God's justice and love.

---

[118] Alex Richardson, "Assess the role played by juridical categories in Orthodox accounts of the atonement with reference to the writings of Georges Florovsky and Vladimir Lossky" (B.A. diss., Oak Hill College, 2010), p 2.

[119] On this aspect of the atonement in Reformed theology see e.g. Letham, *The Work of Christ*, pp 149-155, pp 161-163.

3.5. Salvation: process versus status

Salvation for Orthodoxy means deification. Christ's redemptive work removes the obstacles (sin and death) which prevent the fulfilment of man's vocation of deification given at creation. Lossky writes:

> The way to deification, which was planned for the first man, will be impossible until human nature triumphs over sin and death. The way to union will henceforth be presented to fallen humanity as salvation. This negative term stands for the removal of an obstacle: one is saved from something—from death, and from sin—its root.[120]

Thus, personal application of Christ's work in Orthodoxy makes the fulfilling of mankind's vocation possible. Salvation starts with baptism and chrismation and will be finally and fully achieved after the resurrection of the dead. As such, salvation is orientated to the future event.

One should note here that in Orthodoxy, since Christ's redemptive work only opens the door to fulfilment of man's vocation and since deification depends on human freedom and work, personal application of Christ's work from the viewpoint of achieving salvation puts man in the same position as he had before the fall. That is, in the same manner as before the fall, with deification, there is the risk that mankind will not fulfil his vocation even after Christ's death and resurrection.

In contrast, though salvation in Reformed theology will be completed in the future event of Christ's coming, it is primarily linked to the present status of the believer. Personal application of Christ's redemptive work elevates man to a much higher position than man had before the fall. Through union with Christ, man's sin and Christ's righteousness are interchanged, and so man is declared righteous before God and adopted into God's family. Since these privileges are solely based on Christ's work and they are God's gift,

---

[120]   Lossky, *Mystical Theology*, p 135.

there is no risk of losing them.

3.5.1. *Justification*

Just as some say that Eastern Orthodoxy shares the Western perspective on the atonement but with different emphases, some hold that Orthodoxy also speaks of justification. For example, according to Rommen; 'The Orthodox, taking the gravity of sin seriously, regularly emphasize themes such as sacrifice, atonement, propitiation, and justification.' In support, he then refers to the words from the liturgy used for baptism: 'You are justified. You are illumined. You are sanctified. You are washed: in the Name of our Lord, Jesus Christ, and by the Spirit of our God.'[121]

However, the concepts of justification and righteousness are different in Eastern and Western theology. Justification in Orthodoxy is related to the inner transformation of a person, to the process of deification. This transformation starts with baptism:

> That justifying and sanctifying divine grace which abides in the church is administered by the church to the people by means of the holy mysteries ... baptism and chrismation transmit justifying and regenerating grace.[122]

After these two sacraments, which enable a person to live in union with Christ, inner transformation of a person continues through good works and the Eucharist. The Eucharist is of special significance since through this sacrament, by participation in the real body and blood of Christ, a person partakes in Christ's righteousness. Cabasilas writes: 'Just as we receive from the holy table a Body far superior to our own, the Body of Christ, so in consequence our righteousness becomes a Christ-like righteousness.'[123] In Orthodoxy therefore, one's

---

[121] Edward Rommen, "A Response to Michael Horton," in *Three Views on Eastern Orthodoxy and Evangelicalism* (ed. James J. Stamoolis; Grand Rapids, MI.: Zondervan, 2004), p 155.

[122] Karmaris, "Concerning the Sacraments", pp 21-22.

[123] Nicholas Cabasilas, *The life in Christ* (trans. Carmino J. deCatanzaro; N.Y.: St. Vladimir's Seminary press, 1974), pp 121-122.

righteousness is a real righteousness; a person is actually *made* righteous, rather than *declared* righteous.

This brings several implications for understanding the differences in Reformed and Eastern Orthodox concepts of justification. First, justification in Orthodoxy involves what Reformed theology considers as regeneration and sanctification.

Second, those who belong to the Reformed tradition believe that one is justified by faith alone apart from works. Justification by faith alone is a theme of Romans. In 1:18-3:20 Paul mentions the possibility of obtaining God's righteousness through faith (1:17) and further describes all men as under the power of sin. Then in 3:21-26 he links justification with redemption through Jesus' blood. In 5:1, as the result of our justification, our status before God has changed and so we now have peace with him. Furthermore, we are no longer his enemies and under his wrath; rather we are reconciled to God (5:9-10). Thus, the beginning of the Christian life in the Reformed tradition is marked by God's acceptance.

On the other hand, there are two conditions of justification in the East: the objective condition provided by God through Christ; and the subjective condition which requires man's work. Lossky describes this:

> If God has given us in the Church all the objective conditions, all the means that we need for the attainment of this end [deification], we, on our side, must produce the necessary subjective conditions: for it is in this synergy, in this co-operation of man with God, that the union is fulfilled.[124]

Justification in Orthodoxy thus requires faith, the performance of the church's sacraments, and involves good works.

Finally and crucially, justification in Reformed theology is based on Christ's righteousness which is through union with Christ

---

[124] Lossky, *Mystical Theology*, p 196.

imputed to the individual believer.

In contrast, since in Eastern Orthodox theology one is being made righteous, depending on one's spiritual progress and the obtained level of deification, there are different levels of righteousness and of justification. As Bartos notes; 'It is for this reason, that the state of righteousness could be lost.'[125] Therefore, because of the subjective conditions of justification, no one can be confident about the final result.

3.5.2. Adoption

For the Orthodox, deification parallels adoption. Indeed, there is a link between becoming gods and sons in Psalm 82:6. Just as deification is a process which becomes irreversible only after death,[126] so adoption is also a process. That is, although man becomes a child of God through baptism,[127] at the same time he is on a journey to achieve God's acceptance and thus adoption too.

Russell explains Maximus the Confessor's view on adoption: 'adoption ... is brought about by baptism and is maintained with God's help by the pursuit of the moral life through the practice of the commandments.'[128] Similarly, Thomas describes the connection between spiritual growth and adoption: 'In a spiritual maturity achieved by a mixture of hard work or ascetic struggle and God's grace, we can know God as his friend or as his sons; we can become

---

[125] Bartos, *Deification in Eastern Orthodox Theology*, p 297.

[126] The likeness of God can be lost again due to sin. Irenaeus says; "Having been regained, this item [likeness] can be lost again: when they disobey God, they ruin it, just like our first ancestor did, and thus commit veritable suicide.—*Against Heresies*, 4.39.1 (1109-1110). – cited from Jules Gross, *The Divinization of the Christian according to the Greek Fathers* (trans. Paul A. Onica; Anaheim, California: A&C Press, 2002), 131.

[127] E.g. "It is through baptism that we received remission of sins, sanctification, communion of the Spirit, adoption and life eternal."—Chrysostom, *Homilies on Acts* 14.3 (PG 60.285)—Cited in Karmaris, "Concerning the Sacraments," pp 22-23.

[128] Norman Russell, *The Doctrine of Deification in the Greek Patristic Tradition* (The Oxford Early Christian Studies; Oxford: University Press, 2004), pp 267-68.

children who have God as our inheritance.'[129]

However, since this journey involves both human and divine will, as in the case of justification, no one can be confident about the final result. The believer thus, 'must continuously find himself between fear and hope.'[130] This has an enormous consequence for the relationship with God the Father, who potentially can cease to be Father. For example, Mantzaridis writes:

> The man who believes in Christ, and then loses his faith and rejects his connection with Him, returns to the condition of an unbeliever, burdened now in addition with the tragic responsibility of apostasy. To such a man God ceases to be the "Father," in the special sense of the word, and becomes merely his "Creator." It follows from this that those who, in whatever way, and whatever their responsibility, are estranged from Christ, cannot be considered as having a part in the deifying gift of His resurrection.[131]

On the other hand, adoption in Reformed theology is the outcome of union with Christ. We are declared righteous and accepted into his family at the beginning of our faith. Reformed Christians believe that it is not possible for those who are chosen by the Father and regenerated by the irresistible and sovereign work of the Holy Spirit to lose their salvation or adoption.[132] Moreover, the language of

---

[129] Thomas, *Deification in the Eastern Orthodox Tradition*, p 26.
[130] Stavropoulos, *Partakers of Divine Nature*, p 56.
[131] Mantzaridis, *The Deification of Man*, pp 118-19.
[132] The concept of falling away in Reformed theology is linked to the doctrine of preservation of believers, which follows from the doctrines of election, regeneration and effective calling. That is, if God the Father has elected some men from eternity to be saved, if the work of the Holy Spirit is irresistible and his call is effectual, then believers will be saved. Speaking of perseverance Grudem gives the following formulation: "The perseverance of the saints means that all those who are truly born again will be kept by God's power and will persevere as Christians until the end of their lives, and that only those who persevere until the end have been truly born again."—Grudem, *Systematic Theology*, p 788. Therefore those who are genuine believers, that is, those who are born again will

adoption has the connotation that parents choose whom to adopt, rather than vice versa. Turretin explains that the word "adoption" is derived from the human custom of adoption and notices that an adopter 'receives a stranger into his own family and promises to him paternal favour.' Thus, adoption is a gracious act of our Heavenly Father who wished to adopt us.[133] Indeed, according to the Bible (John 6:37, 40, 44, 65; Psalms 2 and 110) the Father chooses and gives believers to the Son as a gift, and so the Father chooses those whom he adopts. The Orthodox position is however, that the believer does his good work and works out his adoption and so joins the Father in giving himself as a gift to Jesus.

3.6.   Grace: uncreated energy and gift

Both deification in Orthodoxy and union with Christ in the Reformed tradition are achieved by grace. However "grace" has quite distinct meanings in the different traditions. In Orthodox belief, grace is an uncreated energy of God. In the Reformed tradition, grace means that union with Christ, and thus salvation also, is a gift from God. Indeed, there are some passages in the Bible (e.g. 1 Corinthians 15:10 or 2 Corinthians 12:9) which indicate that it is possible to talk about grace in a sense of power or energy of God. Nevertheless, from other passages (e.g. Ephesians 1:5-6 and 2:1-10, Romans 5:2, Titus 2:11) it is clear that grace means that salvation does not depend on good works but is a free gift of God. Salvation is therefore in Reformed theology, an act of the undeserved mercy of God.

Since Orthodoxy does not consider grace as a gift but as a

---

be preserved by God. There are many Bible passages which support the preservation of believers (e.g. John 6:38-40, 10:27-29; Romans 8:30; Ephesians 1:13-14). Nonetheless, there are also other passages which warn of the necessity to continue in the faith (e.g. Colossians 1:21-23; Hebrews 3:12, 6:4-8, 10:26-31). These warnings are addressed to believers and they are means by which God preserves his people. For the relationship between the doctrine of perseverance and the warning passages, see e.g. Berkouwer, *Faith and Perseverance*, pp 110-111.

[133] Turretin, *Institutes of Elenctic Theology*, p 667.

consequence, it also fails to make the distinction between justification and sanctification as described in Reformed theology. Thus, sanctification or the achievement of the likeness of God is the way to salvation. This is not surprising when 2 Peter 1:4, 'that through them you may participate in the divine nature', a foundational verse for deification, is given in the context of obtaining sanctification (2 Peter 1:3-11).

Furthermore, the Orthodox distinction between God's essence and his energies brings confusion as to whether we can know God as he really is. That is, if we can know nothing about God's essence, then we cannot be confident whether his essence corresponds to his energies and his actions towards us or not. Thus, we cannot be sure whether 'God is as he has revealed himself in Jesus Christ.'[134]

3.7. Sacraments

In deification, union with Christ begins through baptism and chrismation. Man is further deified through the Eucharist. Thus, the Church provides the necessary means to achieve salvation through the sacraments, which 'are effectively accomplished independently of the faith of those accepting them.'[135] However, it is important to note that such understanding of the sacraments does not mean that the Orthodox church believes she herself can distribute grace or is in control of the Holy Spirit. Rather, this belief comes from the understanding that the Church is the temple of the Holy Spirit. Meyendorff writes:

> He [The Holy Spirit] never becomes prisoner of the institution, or the personal monopoly of any human being ...

---

[134] Letham, *Through Western Eyes*, p 283.

[135] Karmaris explains the completeness of the sacraments is contingent "upon their divine order and institution by the Lord ... [and] upon the canonical position of the officiating clergy and upon the effect, both *ex opere operato* and *ex opere operantis*."—Karmaris, "Concerning the Sacraments", pp 22-23. However, this does not mean that faith is not important in Orthodoxy.

> It is not the Church which, through the medium of its institutions bestows the Holy Spirit, but it is the Spirit which validates every aspect of Church life, including the institutions.[136]

In Reformed theology union with Christ begins by faith. Faith is closely linked to baptism (Romans 6:3-4, Colossians 2:11-13), which is a sign of faith. Calvin's view of the Eucharist is similar but not the same as the understanding of Eastern Orthodoxy. He says that in the Eucharist, the believer has communion with Christ's physical body:

> I am not satisfied with those persons who, recognizing that we have some communion with Christ, when they would show what it is, make us partakers of the Spirit only, omitting mention of flesh and blood. As though all these things were said in vain: that his flesh is truly food, that his blood is truly drink [John 6:55]; that that none have life except those who eat his flesh and drink his blood [John 6:53]; and other passages pertaining to the same thing![137]

The body of Christ is for Calvin, life-giving: 'The flesh of Christ is like a rich and inexhaustible fountain that pours into us the life springing forth from the Godhead itself.'[138]

However, he maintains that the bread does not literally become the body of Christ: 'But we must establish such a presence of Christ in the Supper as may neither fasten him to the element of bread, nor enclose him in bread, nor circumscribe him in any way.'[139] He further says that 'from the substance of his flesh Christ breathes life into our souls – indeed, pours forth his very life into us – even though Christ's flesh itself does not enter into us.'[140] For Calvin thus, in union with Christ, 'our Mediator is ever present with his own

---

[136] John Meyendorff, *Catholicity and the Church* (Crestwood, New York: St. Vladimir's Seminary Press, 1983), p 28.
[137] Calvin, *Inst.* IV.xvii.7 (2:1366-1367).
[138] Calvin, *Inst.* IV.xvii.9 (2:1369).
[139] Calvin, *Inst.* IV.xvii.19 (2:1381).
[140] Calvin, *Inst.* IV.xvii.32 (2:1404).

people, and in the Supper reveals himself in a special way.'[141]

Therefore, although baptism and the Eucharist in the Reformed tradition correspond to forgiveness of sin and new life in Christ as in Orthodoxy, there are some differences between them. Apart from whether the bread and wine literally become the body and blood of Christ or not, the crucial difference is the role of the sacraments in salvation. As Orthodoxy does not accept that God declares the sinner to be righteous, and so refuses the idea of external juridical decision in salvation, the sacraments are required for salvation. And if the sacraments 'are *necessary for salvation* because they are necessary for *receiving saving grace*, then salvation is really based on faith plus works.'[142] In reformed tradition, salvation is by faith alone and by grace alone. However, we have to remember that because Eastern Orthodoxy considers grace as an energy of God, for the Orthodox believer, there is neither a dichotomy between grace and works nor the question of whether salvation is by faith or works.

3.8. *Predestination*

The Reformed view of union with Christ is rooted in predestination, which Orthodoxy objects to on the basis that it denies human free will. However, predestination is a biblical concept (Ephesians 1:3-14; Romans 8:29-30) and in the Reformed tradition it is balanced with human responsibility, as God's election requires a response on our part. Although this response is elicited by the Holy Spirit, human response is still necessary and is a genuine response.[143] This means that the response can happen at any stage of life, whether a person is young or old. But prior to the response of repentance and faith in Jesus Christ, a person is spiritually dead and under the wrath of God regardless of God's election before the world was made.

---

[141]   Calvin, *Inst.* IV.xvii.30 (2:1403).
[142]   Grudem, *Systematic Theology*, p 973.
[143]   Letham, *The Work of Christ*, p 86.

4.   Conclusion

Comparison and evaluation of the concepts of deification and union with Christ has shown that there are differences in understanding the way of achieving man's salvation, most clearly seen in regard to salvation as a journey earned by human effort, in contrast to a gift given at the beginning of faith. Deification, as chiefly based on only a small number of texts, lacks the more important biblical motifs of Christ's work on the cross as a substitutionary atonement. Furthermore, the Orthodox Church does not accept justification by faith alone. This means that deification does not make a distinction between justification and sanctification; rather justification practically collapses into sanctification. Thus, deification exalts human freedom at the expense of the sovereignty of God.

Nevertheless, deification also has positive aspects from which believers in the Reformed tradition can benefit. These positive features are the stress on personal union with God, the importance of a life of holiness and the emphasis on the whole church as the community where deification takes place. All these features can be lacking in Reformed theology and practice, which emphasises the work of Christ, justification by faith and the need for a personal relationship with God. That is, preoccupation with the benefits of Christ's work, their interrelations and application may leave Christ and a life in personal union with him in the background.[144] Emphasis on justification by faith as crossing the necessary 'line' to achieve salvation can undermine the importance of discipleship. And finally, stress on personal guilt and the need for restoration of relationship with God can bring individualism and an inadequate view of the Church as family.

However, the doctrine of union with Christ, as outlined above, contains all these positive features of deification. Namely, all

---

[144]   Gaffin, "Union with Christ," p 280.

the benefits of Christ's work can be enjoyed only through personal union with Christ; sanctification, that is growing into the image of Christ, is an outcome of the union with Christ and so inseparable from justification; and personal union with Christ means that the believer is in union with others who are part of his body. Thus, the doctrine of union with Christ, fully expounded, should be taught as a balance to the stress on the cross and justification by faith in Reformed churches.

Finally, Orthodox believers can also benefit from the Reformed doctrine of union with Christ. Deification as a means to achieve our human vocation, and thus acceptance by the Father through our good life, can easily lead either into pride, when we think that our spiritual growth is successful, or into despair when we fail to live up to the standards of holiness. Thus, the essential difference between these two concepts is that deification lacks the assurance of salvation and confidence in one's daily walk with God. There are several reasons for this. Firstly, the Orthodox Church does not acknowledge justification by faith alone and so Christ's work is not enough for salvation. Secondly, because of the distinction between God's essence and his energies, confidence in God's character is undermined.

Therefore, what Orthodox believers need to recognize is that God's acceptance is at the beginning of the Christian life rather than at the end. This acceptance is based solely on God's love and mercy expressed through Christ's death and resurrection. As such, acceptance cannot be earned.

Furthermore, there are two important issues when conveying the concept of union with God to Orthodox believers. The first is related to the absence of juridical categories in deification. As Fairbairn helpfully points out, alongside the affirmation of the victory over death and the devil, the focus of explanation should be on God's necessity to punish sin which stems from his holiness.[145] At the same

---

[145] Fairbairn, *Eastern Orthodoxy through Western Eyes*, p 175.

time, it is important to emphasise that Christ's death on the cross is equally the expression of God's love.

And secondly, there is the common misconception by Orthodox people that justification by faith alone is something static, which undermines striving for holiness and spiritual growth (though as noted above, in some cases this could be a real danger and so could be a right objection rather than a misunderstanding.) However, the doctrine of union with Christ is both legal and relational. It holds justification and sanctification as inseparable. It implies both a status (something static) and a personal relationship (something dynamic). Good works and holiness are thus equally as important to the Western Reformed believer as to Orthodox believers.

Nevertheless, outlining the concepts of deification and union with Christ has also shown that there are important similarities between them. Both are grounded in the work and person of Jesus Christ and both refer to the believer's union with his humanity, and through it to the communion with the Triune God. The Holy Spirit is, in both traditions, the one who indwells the believers and applies salvation to them. Likewise, both emphasise the importance of the process of sanctification. Furthermore, likeness to the image of Christ and glorification are the aim of both concepts. No doubt, within both traditions there are believers who love Jesus Christ and glory in him.

Bibliography

St Athanasius. *On the Incarnation.* Translated by A Religious of CSMV. Rev. ed. Crestwood, N.Y.: St Vladimir's Seminary Press, 1993.

Bartos, Emil. *Deification in Eastern Orthodox theology: An Evaluation and Critique of the Theology of Dumitry Staniloae.* Carlisle: Paternoster, 1999.

Berkouwer, G. C. *Faith and Perseverance.* Studies in Dogmatics. Translated by R. D. Knudsen. Grand Rapids: Eerdmans, 1958.

Cabasilas, Nicholas. *The life in Christ.* Translated by Carmino J. deCatanzaro. N.Y.: St. Vladimir's Seminary Press, 1974.

Calvin, John. *Institutes of the Christian Religion.* Edited by John T. McNeill. Translated by Ford Lewis Battles. 2 vols. Library of Christian Classics 20-21. Philadelphia: Westminster, 1960.

Clendenin, Daniel B. *Eastern Orthodox Christianity: A Western Perspective.* Grand Rapids: Baker, 1994.

The Evangelical Alliance Commission on Unity and Truth among Evangelicals (ACUTE). *Evangelicalism and the Orthodox Church.* Carlisle: Paternoster, 2001.

Evans, William B. *Imputation and Impartation: Union with Christ in American Reformed Tradition.* Studies in Christian History and Thought. Milton Keynes: Paternoster, 2008.

Fairbairn, Donald. *Eastern Orthodoxy through Western Eyes.* Louisville, Ky.: Westminster John Knox Press, 2002.

———. *Grace and Christology in the Early Church.* Oxford Early Christian Studies. Oxford: University Press, 2003.

———. "Salvation as Theosis: The teaching of Eastern Theology." *Themelios* Vol 23:3 (1999): pp 42-54.

———. "Patristic soteriology: three trajectories." *Journal of the Evangelical Theological Society* 50/2 (June 2007): pp 289-310.

Florovsky, Georges. *Creation and Redemption.* Vol. 3 of *Collected Works.* Belmont, Mass.: Nordland, 1976.

Gaffin, Richard B. "Union with Christ: some biblical and theological reflections." Pages 271-88 in *Always Reforming: Exploration in systematic theology.* Edited by A.T.B. McGowan. Leicester: IVP, 2006.

Gross, Jules. *The Divinization of the Christian according to the Greek Fathers.* Translated by Paul A. Onica. Anaheim, Ca.: A&C Press, 2002.

Grudem, Wayne. *Systematic Theology: An introduction to Biblical Doctrine.* Leicester: IVP, 1994.

Harper, Michael. *A faith fulfilled: why are Christians across Great Britain embracing Orthodoxy?* Ben Lomond, California: Conciliar Press, 1999.

Hoekema, A.A. *Created in God's Image.* Exeter: Paternoster, 1986.

Karmaris, John. "Concerning the Sacraments." Pages 21-31 in *Eastern Orthodox*

Theology: A Contemporary Reader. 2d ed. Edited by Daniel B. Clendenin. Carlisle: Paternoster, 2003.

Letham, Robert. *Through Western Eyes.* Fearn, Ross-shire: Mentor, 2007.

_____. *The Work of Christ.* Contours of Christian Theology. Downers Grove, Ill.: IVP, 1993.

Lossky, Vladimir. *In the Image and Likeness of God.* Oxford: Mowbray, 1975.

_____. *The Mystical Theology of the Eastern Church.* London: James Clarke and Co., 1957.

_____. *Orthodox Theology: An Introduction.* Translated by Ian and Ihita Kesarcodi-Watson. Crestwood, N.Y.: St. Vladimir's Seminary Press, 1978.

_____. *The Vision of God.* Crestwood, N.Y.: St. Vladimir's Seminary Press, 1983.

Mantzaridis, Georgios I. *The deification of man: St. Gregory Palamas and the Orthodox Tradition.* Translated by Liadain Sherrard. Crestwood, New York: St. Vladimir's Seminary Press, 1984.

Meyendorff, John. *Byzantine theology: Historical Trends and Doctrinal Themes.* Oxford: Mowbrays, 1975.

_____. *Catholicity and the Church.* Crestwood, New York: St. Vladimir's Seminary Press, 1983.

Moo, Douglas S. *The Epistle to the Romans.* The New International Commentary on the New Testament. Cambridge: Eerdmans, 1996.

Mosser, Carl. "The greatest possible blessing: Calvin and deification." *Scottish Journal of Theology* 55 (2002): Pages 36-57.

Murray, John. *Redemption Accomplished and Applied.* London: The Banner of Truth Trust, 1961.

Nellas, Panayiotis. *Deification in Christ: Orthodox Perspectives on the Nature of the Human Person.* Translated by Norman Russell. Crestwood, N.Y.: St Vladimir's Seminary Press, 1987.

Ovey, Mike. *"Application of the Cross Work* (3)." Unpublished Papers - Oak Hill College, 2007.

Reymond, Robert L. *A New Systematic Theology of the Christian Faith.* Rev. and 2d ed. Nashville, Tenn.: Thomas Nelson, 1998.

Richardson, Alex. *"Assess the role played by juridical categories in Orthodox accounts of the atonement with reference to the writings of Georges Florovsky and Vladimir Lossky."* Unpublished B.A. diss., Oak Hill College, 2010.

Rommen, Edward. "A Response to Michael Horton." Pages 155-157 in *Three Views on Eastern Orthodoxy and Evangelicalism.* Edited by James J. Stamoolis. Grand Rapids, MI.: Zondervan, 2004.

Russell, Norman. *The Doctrine of Deification in the Greek Patristic Tradition.* The Oxford Early Christian Studies. Oxford: University Press, 2004.

Stavropoulos, Christoforos. *Partakers of Divine Nature.* Translated by Stanley Harakas. Minneapolis, Minn.: Light and Life, 1976.

Thomas, Stephen. Deification in the Eastern Orthodox Tradition: A Biblical Perspective. Piscataway, N.J.: Gorgias Press, 2007.

Turretin, Francis. *Institutes of Elenctic Theology.* Vol 2. Edited by James T. Dennison. Translated by George Musgrave Giger. Phillipsburg, N.J.: P&R, 1994.

Zernov, Nicolas. *Eastern Christendom: A Study of the Origin and Development of the Eastern Orthodox Church.* Readers Union ed. London: Weidenfeld and Nicolson, 1963.

Ware, Timothy. *The Orthodox Church.* London: Penguin Books, 1969.

Lightning Source UK Ltd.
Milton Keynes UK

177379UK00001B/60/P